ISBN 978-1-5400-1590-7

Visit Hal Leonard Online at
www.halleonard.com

CONTENTS

★ ★ ★ ★ ★ ★ ★ ★ ★ ★ FOREWORD ★ ★ ★ ★ ★ ★ ★ ★ ★ ★
by Merle Haggard

Not too long ago, I was trying to learn a Bob Wills-style fiddle tune – I think it was "Durang's Hornpipe" – and just couldn't seem to get certain parts of it. I asked Tiny Moore to write down the tune to see if we could learn it that way. He did, and we did learn the tune. I got to thinking that there probably are a lot of people who can read music and might like to learn some of these songs and styles. That is the reason for this book.

My music-reading ability is very limited. Tiny Moore's skill to read and write music has made it easier to pick up songs I probably never would have learned if he hadn't written down some of the old Wills tunes we had on the band bus. We listened to them many times, but there are some things that are almost impossible for the ear to determine. That is the primary reason for style difference in this book, because many fiddlers have learned by ear, and different people may hear and play a phrase of a song differently.

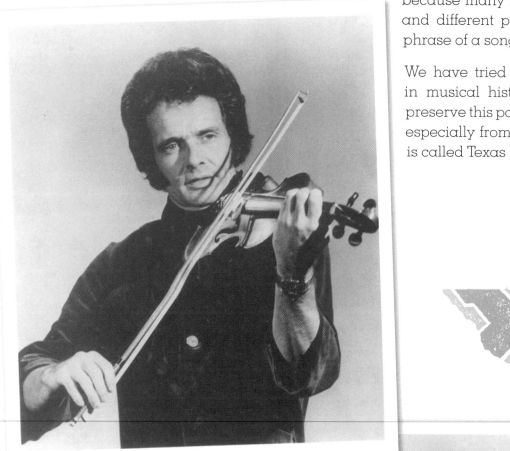

We have tried in this book to put this time in musical history down on paper and to preserve this part of American fiddle playing, especially from the midwest U.S.A. The style is called Texas Fiddlin'.

–Merle Haggard

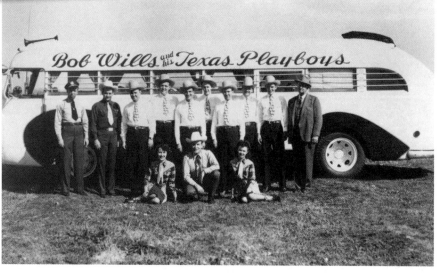

★ ★ ★ ★ ★ ★ ★ INTRODUCTION ★ ★ ★ ★ ★ ★ ★

by Tiny Moore

Swinging Texas Fiddle playing probably started with Bob Wills in the 1920s. Bob's dad, Uncle John, and some of Bob's uncles on the Foley side of the family taught Bob most of his fiddle tunes. But somewhere along the line, Bob started changing a few phrases or "licks" to fit what he felt like playing. Since Bob was greatly influenced by traditional jazz, he began incorporating some of this "feel" into his breakdowns. When Bob Wills played a breakdown, it would "swing." It made people want to tap their feet and start dancing.

I had the honor of playing with Bob Wills from 1946 to 1950, and continued to work for him until 1955 at Wills Point, Sacramento, California. The Bob Wills style used in this book is as I remember him playing these tunes on the bandstand.

I grew up in central and south Texas and have always enjoyed playing string band music. My first gig was at a farmhouse in Energy, Texas, performing with my Uncle Jim Baskin. I made 75 cents for that effort. In this book is the first breakdown I ever learned. I call it "Uncle Jim" because he taught it to me and I don't know its real name. My mother, Uncle Jim, I, and a few others played for school shows and the like in Hamilton and Comanche counties.

I wasn't too interested in breakdown fiddle until about 1973, when I got a call from Merle Haggard to work for him. Hag rekindled my interest in the instrument. For that, and many other things, I thank him. I spent three enjoyable years with him on the road. During that time, he came up with the idea for this book.

Merle has been interested in the fiddle for a long time, but he really took up learning to play it about 1970. By the time I joined him in 1973, he was already using the fiddle in his concerts and on records. His grandad, John Haggard, was a well-known fiddler in Arkansas and Oklahoma.

Merle's first choice of a fiddler to use in showing a style was Vernon Solomon, Grand Masters National Fiddle Champion in 1972. A better choice could not have been made, but more about Vernon later. Then, to show a change in styles, we decided also to use Warren Helton from Missouri. And as an added attraction, we asked Johnny Gimble to play a tune for us in his style.

In this book, you will find several duplications of tunes. Notice, however, that each one sounds different. Most fiddlers learn tunes by listening to others, and each hears a phrase or lick differently; also, some fiddlers add licks to the tune, giving it a different flavor. While it is impossible to get the "feel" of this music down on paper, a combination of playing the notes and listening to recordings and other fiddlers should give the desired result.

To our knowledge, these versions of the breakdowns are not in print anywhere else. We hope they will be enjoyed by many people. And with a profusion of young people interested in the fiddle, we trust this book will help keep Swinging Texas Fiddlin' alive.

–Tiny Moore

★ ★ ★ ★ CHORDS & FIDDLE BOWING ★ ★ ★ ★

The chord names shown represent only one way of harmonizing these tunes. Some guitar players may have different ideas; that's just part of breakdown fiddle playing.

The chord progressions used by several guitar players for standard breakdowns is almost a jazz concept. For an eight-bar phrase, it would look like this:

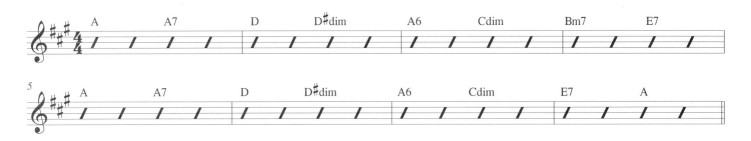

Again, the chords shown here are only suggestions, not necessarily indicating the way they must be played. Every fiddler has his own concept of how the breakdowns should sound and may want to use different chords from those shown. This practice is perfectly acceptable.

Songs that will fit the progression above are "Grey Eagle," "Sally Goodin'," "Uncle Jim," "Sally Johnson" (transpose the progression to G and use for the standard part of the song), "Leather Britches," and "Bill Cheatham." There are many others also.

Playing the Swinging Texas Fiddle should not be a "tied down" thing, but should allow both fiddler and accompanist to use their imagination. The fiddle bowing can also be different from what is shown. Most of the contest players prefer to use a lot of single-note bow strokes. When using this method try to start each measure with a down stroke, and accent very slightly each down stroke of the bow. Of course, you may have to use slurs not shown here to make your bowing come out right. If you are after the old-fashioned hoedown sound, you can use the double-shuffle type of bowing on most of the fast songs. It is all a matter of choice. Double shuffle is bowed like this:

★ ★ ★ ★ ★ VERNON SOLOMON STYLE ★ ★ ★ ★ ★

Instead of saving the best for last, we are going to give you the best right off the bat. The first section of songs is in the style of Vernon Solomon, the 1972 Grand Masters Fiddling Champion. This is the style – along with some of the songs – that won him the title.

Vernon was born in Kauffman County, Texas, and comes from a long line of fiddlers. His father Irvin was, in Vernon's estimation, the best breakdown fiddler he ever heard. Pleasant Reilly (known as Hap), the Solomon boys' grandfather, was also a popular fiddler. Anyone familiar with Texas fiddlers knows that Vernon's brother Norman can fiddle with the best.

When Vernon was four or five years old, his dad tried to help him learn to play the fiddle, but it didn't work out. Mr. Solomon finally said that if his boy was going to learn to play, he would have to do it on his own. Vernon's grandad gave him a fiddle made of boardark. Just before he was five, Vernon was sitting on an apple box on the back porch while his mother was washing clothes on a rub board, and something happened that Vernon can't explain. He just started playing "Bully of the Town." It was a big thrill, even for a five-year-old. Thus began the fiddling of one of the best ever to come along. It has been many years since that happened, but the experience has stuck vividly in his mind. His kids started playing about the same way.

Vernon now lives in Thome, Texas, about 25 miles north of Fort Worth. Three of his songs that are nearest to his heart are included in this book: "Sally Johnson," "Leather Britches," and "Sally Goodin'."

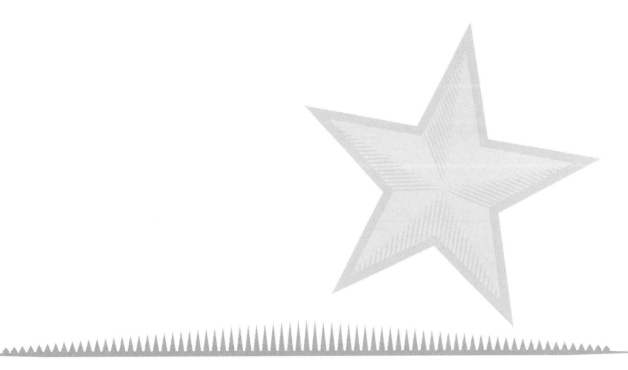

Sally Johnson

Grey Eagle

Leather Britches

Sally Goodin'

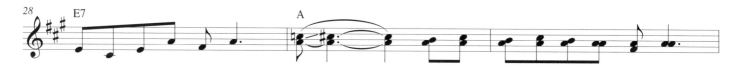

Done Gone

1.
Gm

2.
Gm

D.S. al Coda

CODA

33
Gm

Dusty Miller

D.S. al Coda
(take 1st ending)

Waggoner

Love a Nobody

Black and White Rag

Dubre Waltz

Ragtime Annie

Shannon Waltz

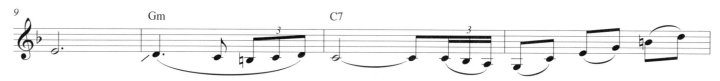

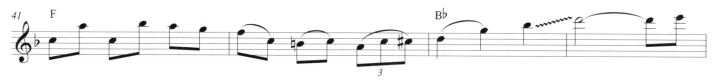

★ ★ ★ ★ ★ ★ BOB WILLS STYLE ★ ★ ★ ★ ★ ★

Here, in the "heart" of the Texas fiddling book, is the style that probably started it all: the style of Bob Wills. So much has been written about this man that I am not going to try to add to it.

I enjoyed working with him in the Texas Playboys for several years, and these tunes are as I remember him playing them. It is hard to get the "feel" of his playing, but by performing what is here and listening to recordings, you will get, I hope, the right "feel."

Sally Johnson

Don't Let the Deal Go Down

Twinkle, Twinkle, Little Star

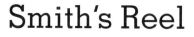

Smith's Reel

Little Betty Brown

Durang's Hornpipe

Arkansas Traveler

Liberty

Hoppin' Lucy

Paddy on the Turnpike

★ ★ ★ ★ ★ UNCLE JIM BASKIN ★ ★ ★ ★ ★

I call this tune "Uncle Jim" because I don't know its real name. My uncle, Jim Baskin, from Hamilton and Comanche counties in Texas, taught me this melody. It is the first breakdown I ever learned, so I had to include it in this book.

Uncle Jim

★ ★ ★ ★ JOHNNY GIMBLE VERSION ★ ★ ★ ★

The great Johnny Gimble probably is one of the best – and best-known – fiddlers in the country today. He's a studio musician, living in Austin, Texas. John sent me this version of "Bill Cheatham," and I think it is outstanding. I hope you enjoy Gimble's arrangement of the tune.

Bill Cheatham

WARREN HELTON STYLE

★ ★ ★ ★   ★ ★ ★ ★

The final section of this book contains versions of fiddle tunes by Warren Helton, a third-generation (at least) fiddler from Vienna, Missouri. His grandfather, Gib Helton, was a well-respected player who passed the fiddle knowledge on to his son Vernon. Vernon, Warren's father, started teaching him to play when Warren was about nine years old. Warren is one of four fiddling brothers; their uncle, George Helton, was still fiddling at age 84. Big Howdy Forrester was always Warren's favorite fiddler, and he was not alone in that opinion.

In comparing the styles of Vernon Solomon and Warren Helton, it might be said that Warren's style is the link between Texas and Tennessee. The first tune, "Waldo," comes from the Helton family of at least three generations ago. A fiddler named Waldo Helton first played it. Warren has heard a similar tune called "Red Bird."

Waldo

Bill Cheatham

Sally Goodin'

Grey Eagle

Ragtime Annie

Texas Picnic

Leather Britches

Katy Hill

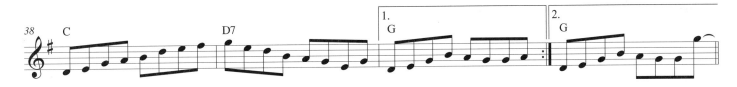

Billy in the Low Ground

Wednesday Night Waltz

HAL•LEONARD® VIOLIN PLAY-ALONG

The Violin Play-Along Series

Play your favorite songs quickly and easily!

Just follow the music, listen to the CD or online audio to hear how the violin should sound, and then play along using the separate backing tracks. The audio files are enhanced so you can adjust the recordings to any tempo without changing pitch!

1. Bluegrass
00842152 ....$14.99

2. Popular Songs
00842153 ....$14.99

3. Classical
00842154 ....$14.99

4. Celtic
00842155 ....$14.99

5. Christmas Carols
00842156 ....$14.99

6. Holiday Hits
00842157 ....$14.99

7. Jazz
00842196 ....$14.99

8. Country Classics
00842230 ....$12.99

9. Country Hits
00842231 ....$14.99

10. Bluegrass Favorites
00842232 ....$14.99

11. Bluegrass Classics
00842233 ....$14.99

12. Wedding Classics
00842324 ....$14.99

13. Wedding Favorites
00842325 ....$14.99

14. Blues Classics
00842427 ....$14.99

15. Stephane Grappelli
00842428 ....$14.99

16. Folk Songs
00842429 ....$14.99

17. Christmas Favorites
00842478 ....$14.99

18. Fiddle Hymns
00842499 ....$14.99

19. Lennon & McCartney
00842564 ....$14.99

20. Irish Tunes
00842565 ....$14.99

21. Andrew Lloyd Webber
00842566 ....$14.99

22. Broadway Hits
00842567 ....$14.99

23. Pirates of the Caribbean
00842625 ....$14.99

24. Rock Classics
00842640 ....$14.99

25. Classical Masterpieces
00842642 ....$14.99

26. Elementary Classics
00842643 ....$14.99

27. Classical Favorites
00842646 ....$14.99

28. Classical Treasures
00842647 ....$14.99

29. Disney Favorites
00842648 ....$14.99

30. Disney Hits
00842649 ....$14.99

31. Movie Themes
00842706 ....$14.99

32. Favorite Christmas Songs
00102110 ....$14.99

33. Hoedown
00102161 ....$14.99

34. Barn Dance
00102568 ....$14.99

35. Lindsey Stirling
00109715 ....$19.99

36. Hot Jazz
00110373 ....$14.99

37. Taylor Swift
00116361 ....$14.99

38. John Williams
00116367 ....$14.99

39. Italian Songs
00116368 ....$14.99

40. Trans-Siberian Orchestra
00119909.................$19.99

41. Johann Strauss
00121041 ....$14.99

42. Light Classics
00121935 ....$14.99

43. Light Orchestra Pop
00122126 ....$14.99

44. French Songs
00122123 ....$14.99

45. Lindsey Stirling Hits
00123128 ....$19.99

46. Piazzolla Tangos
48022997 ....$16.99

47. Light Masterworks
00124149 ....$14.99

48. Frozen
00126478 ....$14.99

49. Pop/Rock
00130216 ....$14.99

50. Songs for Beginners
00131417 ....$14.99

51. Chart Hits for Beginners
00131418 ....$14.99

52. Celtic Rock
00148756 ....$14.99

53. Rockin' Classics
00148768 ....$14.99

54. Scottish Folksongs
00148779 ....$14.99

55. Wicked
00148780 ....$14.99

56. The Sound of Music
00148782 ....$14.99

57. Movie Music
00150962 ....$14.99

58. The Piano Guys – Wonders
00151837 ....$19.99

59. Worship Favorites
00152534.................$14.99

60. The Beatles
00155293 ....$14.99

61. Star Wars: The Force Awakens
00157648 ....$14.99

62. Star Wars
00157650 ....$14.99

63. George Gershwin
00159612.................$14.99

64. Lindsey Stirling Favorites
00159634.................$19.99

65. Taylor Davis
00190208.................$19.99

66. Pop Covers
00194642.................$14.99

67. Love Songs
00211896.................$14.99

68. Queen
00221964.................$14.99

69. La La Land
00232247.................$17.99

71. Andrew Lloyd Webber Hits
00244688.................$14.99

72. Lindsey Stirling – Selections from Warmer in the Winter
00254923.................$19.99

74. The Piano Guys – Christmas Together
00262873.................$19.99

7777 W. BLUEMOUND RD. P.O. BOX 13819 MILWAUKEE, WI 53213

www.halleonard.com

0218

VIOLIN DUET
COLLECTIONS

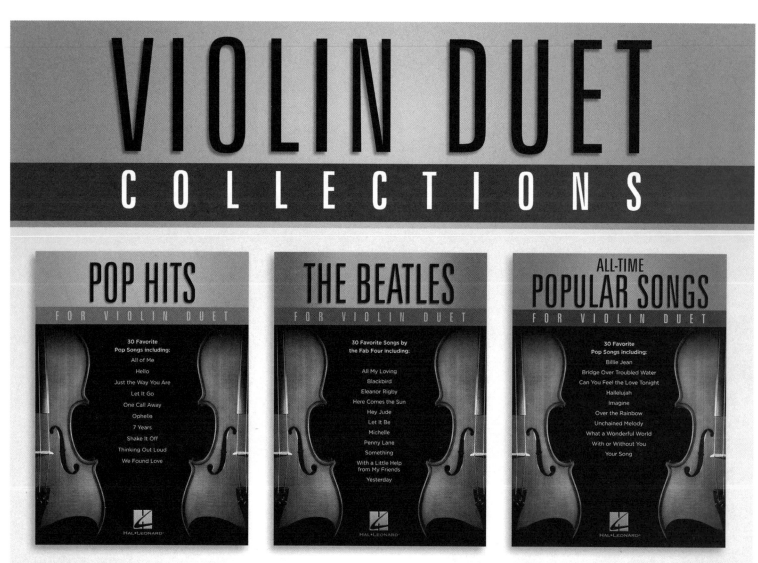

These collections are designed for violinists familiar with first position and comfortable reading basic rhythms. Each two-page arrangement includes a violin 1 and violin 2 part, with each taking a turn at playing the melody for a fun and challenging ensemble experience.

ALL-TIME POPULAR SONGS FOR VIOLIN DUET

Billie Jean • Bridge over Troubled Water • Can You Feel the Love Tonight • Hallelujah • Imagine • Over the Rainbow • Unchained Melody • What a Wonderful World • With or Without You • Your Song and more.

00222449 . . . . $12.99

THE BEATLES FOR VIOLIN DUET

All My Loving • Blackbird • Eleanor Rigby • A Hard Day's Night • Hey Jude • Let It Be • Michelle • Ob-La-Di, Ob-La-Da • Something • When I'm Sixty-Four • Yesterday and more.

00218245 . . . . $12.99

POP HITS FOR VIOLIN DUET

All of Me • Hello • Just the Way You Are • Let It Go • Love Yourself • Ophelia • Riptide • Say Something • Shake It Off • Story of My Life • Take Me to Church • Thinking Out Loud • Wake Me Up! and more.

00217577 . . . . $12.99

DISNEY SONGS FOR VIOLIN DUET

Beauty and the Beast • Can You Feel the Love Tonight • Colors of the Wind • Do You Want to Build a Snowman? • Hakuna Matata • How Far I'll Go • I'm Wishing • Let It Go • Some Day My Prince Will Come • A Spoonful of Sugar • Under the Sea • When She Loved Me • A Whole New World and more.

00217578 . . . . $12.99

HAL•LEONARD®

www.halleonard.com

Prices, contents, and availability subject to change without notice.

0617